He Came Through Drippin'

He Came Through Drippin'

My son, Chandler Bailey, has a unique way of articulating and applying biblical truths to our daily lives. Through this devotional, you will be encouraged and inspired to face and embrace every daily challenge with the faith, confidence, and assurance that Jesus died and rose for us to operate in.

>Bishop Herbert Bailey
>Senior Pastor
>Right Direction Church Int'l,
>Columbia, SC

Chandler Bailey's new devotional, "He Came Through Dripping," will encourage you in your daily walk with Jesus. I watched my son win many battles, walk victory, and grow into the man that he is now. That's the power of the blood of Jesus! Wherever you may be in your walk with the Lord. I am very proud of my son and the work he has done to be where he is now. I know this devotional will heal, help, deliver, and bless many.

>Dr. Marcia Bailey
>Co-pastor of Right Direction Church International

He Came Through Drippin'

He Came Through Drippin'

Others Works:

Happy Faith Everyday 7-Day Devotional

Chandler Bailey Media, LLP

Kingdom Muzik Entertainment, LLC

Co-Visionary - Kingdom Business Network

He Came Through Drippin'

CHANDLER BAILEY
Media

Chandler Bailey Media, LLP Presents:

He Came Through Drippin'
30 Day Devotional

Chandler S. Bailey

He Came Through Drippin'

He Came Through Drippin'

Copyright © 2024 Chandler Bailey Media, LLP

All rights reserved. No part of this book may be reproduced in any form without permission of the author and/or publisher.

References:

The Holy Bible AMP

The Holy Bible NIV

The Holy Bible KJV

The Holy Bible NKJV

The Holy Bible NLT

The Holy Bible Passion Translation

He Came Through Drippin'

He Came Through Drippin'

Day 1
Jesus the Carrier

"Cast all your anxiety on him because He cares for you." Peter 5:7

Faith Fam, today I want you to focus your faith on the fact that God isn't just someone we cast our cares on; He also carries us through the storms. It was a recent Sunday when I came into the church feeling the full weight of leadership and bearing the responsibilities of life, ministry, and more. During that Sunday's worship, I felt crushed, and then I heard God's still, small voice say, "I know you feel the pressure, but I trust what I'm squeezing out of you."

He Came Through Drippin'

It was at that point I totally surrendered to God. He helped me understand that the more He instills in me, the more He allows life to draw out of me. So today, don't complain. Allow God to shift your focus from pressure to promise, and you'll find you have everything you need and more along the journey. Keep the faith!

What do you need to let God carry today?

What area of your life do you need to surrender to God?

Write down a list of areas of pressure in your life.

"The only way you will last is if you cast"
— **C.S. Bailey**

He Came Through Drippin'

He Came Through Drippin'

Day 2
Delight

Psalms 37:4 - Delight thyself also in the LORD, and he shall give thee the desires of thine heart.

In light of today's priorities and the goals that many of us have. Have you ever wondered why many of our dreams and the desires of our hearts don't always come past? Many believers do not experience God's glory because we hang on to our perspectives and desires. Today God wants to give you the desires of your heart. Faith fam, it all starts here. Don't worry about having tangible proof that God is moving in your life. Allow the Lord to minister to you from his heart to yours. When you allow God to deal with you; heart to heart, then you can be trusted to work with God; hand to hand. Faith fam, I want you to experience more than enough blessings from God, but it all starts with us making God more than enough in life.

What are your priorities today?

What goals do you need God's help for today?

What negative outlooks/perspectives do you need to let go of today?

"Sometimes you have to let go of the let go's"
– C.S. Bailey

He Came Through Drippin'

He Came Through Drippin'

Day 3
Commit to the Lord Pt. 1

"Commit thy way unto the LORD; trust also in him; and he shall bring it to pass." Psalms 37:5

I encourage you today to take all of your plans and all of your thoughts to God. It is here that the scripture of fully committing our desires and thoughts to the Lord is so important. However, the word of God doesn't just tell us to commit; it also encourages us to trust. Faith fam trusting in the Lord is not truly trusting in the Lord if it includes your timeline. Today, I want you to trade your schedule for the ways of the Lord and to exchange the focus of your timeline for the trust of the Lord. Keep the Faith!

How can you trust God more today?

What expectations do you have that involve time and it happens on your terms that you need to give back to God?

Write down a summary of how you can decide today and, in the future, to trust more in God.

"Take it all to him and watch him give right back to you better" – **C.S. Bailey**

He Came Through Drippin'

He Came Through Drippin'

Day 4
Commit to the Lord Pt. 2

"For where your treasure is, there will your heart be also." Matthew 6:21

Today, I want you to weigh and contrast your desires and what you need from God from your pure need of the Lord in your everyday walk-in life. Do we truly value the things of the Lord? My wife Audria and I are currently openly believing in God for the right timing of the Lord to purchase or get blessed with a new home! We have outgrown our house and, with our third child, Hero, who's running around and climbing everywhere, we desire a bigger kitchen, closet space, laundry area, a playroom for the kids, and larger bedrooms and hosting and sitting rooms.

However, I can tell you I don't want this more than I want God to have his way in my desire for the next. Faith fam, this is what I mean in the scripture emphasis today. Do you want more from God than you want "in" God? So today, place your treasure in the one who holds the world and watch your heart connect with God's timing and the desires He has for you, never like before!

What aspect of your relationship with the Lord do you cherish the most?

If God didn't do anything else what area of your life would you be the most grateful for?

"The only way you will last is if you cast."
— **C.S. Bailey**

He Came Through Drippin'

He Came Through Drippin'

Day 5
The Heart of Servant Leadership

"But he that is greatest among you shall be your servant. [12] And whosoever shall exalt himself shall be abased, and; and he that shall humble himself shall be exalted." Matthew 23:11-12 KJV

In a world that often glorifies self-promotion and personal success, let's turn our attention to a different kind of leadership: servant leadership. The key to greatness in the Kingdom is found in serving others, as Jesus taught in Matthew 23:11-12.

But he that is greatest among you shall be your servant. [12] And whosoever shall exalt himself shall be abased, and; and he that shall humble

He Came Through Drippin'

himself shall be exalted." This powerful scripture reminds us that true success and elevation come from a place of humility and service to others. So today, let's choose to lead with a spirit of giving rather than focusing on receiving. Together, we can redefine success and create a lasting impact in the lives of those around us.

How could you serve others in general better in your life?

What are some gifts you have that, if given the opportunity would bless others greatly?

> *"The only reason you have strategy is because God can trust you with the crazy."*
> **– C.S. Bailey**

He Came Through Drippin'

He Came Through Drippin'

Day 6
Make the Heart Connect

So above all, guard the affections of your heart, for they affect all that you are. Pay attention to the welfare of your innermost being, for from there flows the wellspring of life. Proverbs 4:23 The Passion Translation

IF GOD GETS YOUR HEART,

EVERYTHING ELSE WILL FOLLOW...

God has pressed upon my Spirit that He desires to connect with our hearts. Therefore, during dark times and tough seasons, our faith should leap into the arms of God. When we allow God to make the heart connect, we demonstrate trust in our relationship with God. If you make mistakes, let me tell you this. God is less moved by our flesh but more interested in the movement of our hearts. If we truly give God our hearts and connect with God like he is drawing us, then everything else will follow.

How can you continue to give God your heart today?

What has gotten in your heart that should not be there?

What are some things starting today that you need to protect from having access to your heart?

"If God gets your heart, everything else will fall into place" – **C.S. Bailey**

He Came Through Drippin'

He Came Through Drippin'

Day 7
Renewed Strength

"But those who hope in the Lord will renew their strength. They will soar on wings like eagles; they will run and not grow weary; they will walk and not be faint." Isaiah 40:31

I get it; it's easy to give up hope and feel mentally tired, physically drained, and even spiritually empty some days. However, I believe your faith is like a fecund tree, ready to sprout any day. As you patiently learn God's decrees and understand His ultimate will for your life, don't let the hustle and bustle of your day conspire against God's word planted in the fecund soil of your heart. Allow God to renew your strength. Today, Faith Fam, stand firm and keep the faith. Remember, you have what it takes, and what it takes is your unwavering faith in God's promises!

Let's brain dump everything that is draining you right now… "no worries I'll wait"

How can you prepare, plan, and posture yourself better to have better days in the future?

"It may be happening around you but it doesn't have to happen in you" – **C.S. Bailey**

He Came Through Drippin'

He Came Through Drippin'

_____

_____

_____

_____

_____

_____

_____

_____

_____

_____

_____

_____

Day 8
Faith IN' God, not just 'Faith FOR

Hey Faith Fam,

Today, I want to emphasize the concept of having 'Faith IN' God, not just 'Faith FOR' specific outcomes. Jeremiah 33:3 tells us, "Call to me, and I will answer you and tell you great and unsearchable things you do not know." We should have faith in God's character and nature, which will never change, rather than putting all our focus on the things we want to see happen. I encourage you to develop a deep-rooted 'Faith IN' God. Believe in His wisdom, timing, and plan for your life.

How can you trust in God's timing better today?

What does a deep-rooted faith in trusting in the Lord mean to you?

Write down a list of descriptions of God's character to build your faith. GOD is...

"We must have Faith IN not just Faith FOR."
— **C.S. Bailey**

He Came Through Drippin'

He Came Through Drippin'

Day 9

Anointed for Alignment: Living in Purposeful Faith

Good day, Faith Fam!

I want you to know you're anointed, not just appointed. We often accept assignments without recognizing that God placed us there because of an alignment. So today, focus your faith on the fact that you're not just assigned—you're anointed.

You see, we often need clarification on whether we're the right person for the job simply because we hold the position. We question whether we're powerful enough. But remember, God does not appoint someone He hasn't already chosen. So today, whatever your role, whatever you're doing in life, remember you're not just in an assignment—you're anointed for the work.

Write down a declaration encouraging yourself in the Lord about why God picked you for your assignment.

What areas of your personal life or profession do you doubt?

"Being anointed for what's next means you're called for what's now." - **C.S. Bailey**

He Came Through Drippin'

He Came Through Drippin'

Day 10
Don't Toil Use Your Oil

"The Spirit of the Lord GOD is upon Me Because the LORD has anointed Me To preach good tidings to the poor; He has sent Me to heal the brokenhearted, To proclaim liberty to the captives, And the opening of the prison to those who are bound." Isaiah 61:1 (NKJV)

What's up, Faith Fam! I am delighted to get your day moving with this robust concept that God has given me just for you. Today, I want you to ponder what is required for you to go to the next level. Once you do that, I want you to embrace my argument that, for us to go to the next level, we are going to have to stand out from the rest. However, the problem lies within the unpacking of this question: How are you going to get better when everyone is getting better too? And how are we going to measure our success without comparing ourselves with one another?

This is what you're going to do. Are you ready? Make sure you write this down! You will work from oil, with oil, towards oil (oil = anointing). See, Faith Fam, if you want to have "good success" (God's version of success), you will have to dip your entire process, from start to finish, in "oil." You want to seize every opportunity with the oil of God. This is how you're going to get the job done and maximize your grind. So today, don't toil; use your oil and watch God take you from here to there as you ask Him to anoint your start, strategy, and

He Came Through Drippin'

finish. If you do this, Faith Fam, you will have the anointing to maximize your grind.

What areas of your life have you honestly compared yourself with others in?

How could you use your oil/anointing/gifting better in your life?

What are some areas in your life you've been working too hard/toiling in?

"Get more done in life by using your oil"
— **C.S. Bailey**

He Came Through Drippin'

He Came Through Drippin'

Day 11
On God!

"Casting all your care upon him; for He careth for you." 1 Peter 5:7 KJV

I haven't been keeping up with my favorite Christian hip-hop artists as I used to. LOL, Lord help me; I hope I'm not losing touch with the culture of young people and trendy music like hip-hop. However, I recently discovered an artist named Limoblaze, a Christian Afro artist signed to Reach Records! The point is, he has this song, "Put it ON God," and it has been life-changing when I tap into the strength of the Lord.

So today, what do you need to put on God? What have you been holding onto that you

He Came Through Drippin'

haven't cast your cares and WORRIES on the Lord? If you've been carrying your weight, pain, and more, maybe it's because you won't let go and let God. I know all these things may sound cliché, but you genuinely need to hear them, faith fam! It's time to stop doing things your way. Look how far that has gotten you. It has taken you nowhere, and God is trying to bring you to new places. What am I saying? You hold onto the weight, and not laying it aside is slowing you down, and God can't take you to the places and seasons He has for you unless you're lighter. Today, let's cast our cares on the KING, who can lift us up and into new territories. Let's get there.

He Came Through Drippin'

How could you cast your cares unto the Lord better today?

What have you been holding onto that you haven't cast your cares and WORRIES on the Lord?

Write down a list of names of people who could stand and pray with you in these areas.

"Why carry what He's caring for?"
– **C.S. Bailey**

He Came Through Drippin'

He Came Through Drippin'

He Came Through Drippin'

Day 12
The Power to Keep Going

"That is why we never give up. Though our bodies are dying, our spirits are being renewed every day. 17 For our present troubles are small and won't last very long. Yet they produce for us a glory that vastly outweighs them and will last forever! 18 So we don't look at the troubles we can see now; rather, we fix our gaze on things that cannot be seen. For the things we see now will soon be gone, but the things we cannot see will last forever."
2 Corinthians 4:16-18 16 NLT

There will be days when you feel like quitting and giving up. During these moments of potential failure, don't let the negative thoughts and mental breakdowns keep you from recognizing the significance of how far you've come and where you're going. My friend, let me

He Came Through Drippin'

ask you wholeheartedly, do you know the power you possess when you immerse yourself in God's presence? I want you to emerge from this storm drenched in God's power! I often think of Shadrach, Meshach, and Abednego, who were thrown into the fiery furnace (Daniel 3:16-18). I believe the reason they were not burned up is because they were soaked in God's presence. So today, put on the whole armor of God, decree and declare over your mind that you have the mind of Christ, and let the presence of God saturate your day. I can't wait to share more about the supernatural saturation protocol God has for you and your prayer life.

He Came Through Drippin'

What areas of your life do you feel like giving up in?

What are some ways you can take advantage of and make time for the presence of the Lord in your life?

"You have to keep it on you as you keep on keeping on." **- C.S. Bailey**

He Came Through Drippin'

He Came Through Drippin'

Day 13
Strength of My Life

The Lord is my strength and my shield; My heart trusted in Him, and I am helped; Therefore my heart greatly rejoices, And with my song, I will praise Him. 8 The Lord is their strength, And He is the saving refuge of His anointed. 9 Save Your people, And bless Your inheritance; Shepherd them also, And bear them up forever." Psalms 28:7-9 NKJV

Today, I want you to walk in the strength of the Lord. Don't worry about how much energy you have or whether you know exactly what to do. Instead, lean into God and soak in His strength. When you do this, you will become a vessel He can fill with His power. Today, focus on God providing everything you need for your day. Don't let life's demands or the distractions of

He Came Through Drippin'

current crises keep you from absorbing and embracing the strength of the Lord in your life. So today, don't just keep the faith—walk with the faith. When you do, you'll experience power in Christ and in life like never before! Say this prayer with me: Holy Spirit, I need you! I need you to infuse me with the strength of the Lord. I can't walk, go, or think without your shielding presence in my day. Spirit of the living Lord, go before me, walk next to me, and protect me from behind. I trust you and know that today will be good, and I will see your hand in the land of the living! It is in your name I pray, Jesus. Amen!

He Came Through Drippin'

Today how can you walk more in the strength of the Lord?

Write down various worries, concerns, or things going on in your life that you lack understanding in.

"You don't have to know why to acknowledge that God already knows what's going on."
- **C.S. Bailey**

He Came Through Drippin'

He Came Through Drippin'

Day 14
Faith for the Overflow

"Now to him who can do immeasurably more than all we ask or imagine, according to his power that is at work within us" Ephesians 3:20 NIV

If you believe you're believing for more, why not stretch it to more than enough in your expectations? We can see in scripture that the oil ran out when the number of vessels ran out. Please center your thoughts on defining biblically that those vessels represent the creative expression of opportunity. Suppose you can have faith in the endless possibilities God has for you. In that case, you can receive the faithfulness of God's divine empowerment to

He Came Through Drippin'

receive the overflow He has for your life. So, stretch your faith, because when you are not, you are not hurting anything but yourself. Faith Fam, I want you to imagine the endless opportunities God has for you. Today, target your faith in the knowledge that God is faithful to give you the oil that will not run out for you. Today, experience the overflow that He has for you!

What are some areas of your life that you can stretch for more in?

What are some areas of your life that you can or are believing for overflow in?

Encourage yourself in the Lord and write about the goodness of the Lord and how HE has been faithful in your life.

"GOD can do it, you know."
- Chandler Righteous Bailey

He Came Through Drippin'

He Came Through Drippin'

Day 15
A Glory Mindset

"Do not conform to the pattern of this world, but be transformed by renewing your mind. Then you will be able to test and approve what God's will is—his good, pleasing, and perfect will." Romans 12:2

Faith fam, I believe a transformed mind is the key to unlocking your royal potential. Here are some practical steps to renew your thoughts and align your mindset with God's vision for your life. Have you considered what thoughts or beliefs have prevented you from living out your royal identity in Christ?

Being a creative and spontaneous individual, my friends often referred to me as "random" while growing up. However, I have managed to transform this trait into a powerful tool for my ministry assignment. How did I achieve this? The answer lies in my mindset. A renewed mindset holds immense power; it enables us to experience greater freedom and joy in our walk with God.

Today let's be intentional in cultivating spiritual growth and make a daily habit of meditating on God's Word, which will fill your mind with His truth and promises.

Write down and research 3-5 scriptures that you can depend on to boost your confidence in your transformational value.

Say this guided prayer:

Heavenly Father, help me to grow spiritually by meditating on Your Word daily and embracing

He Came Through Drippin'

gratitude. Guide me in replacing negative thoughts with Scripture-based affirmations. Show me areas of my thought life needing improvement and lead me to relevant Bible verses. Provide a trusted friend or mentor for support and encouragement as I renew my mind. May my growth bring honor to Your name. In Jesus' name, I pray. Amen!

"We want to do what He is doing, go where He is taking, and say what He is saying."
— **C.S. Bailey**

He Came Through Drippin'

He Came Through Drippin'

Day 16
Postured for The Promise

"For all of God's promises have been fulfilled in Christ with a resounding "Yes!" And through Christ, our "Amen" (which means "Yes") ascends to God for his glory." 2 Corinthians 1:20 NLT

Faith Fam, I want to encourage you to reflect on how your posture has been toward the things of God. Will you still say yes to God though it looks like manifestation has not arrived yet? A "still-yes" is a posture of agreement that says, even if things are not happening well around you, you keep your faith that God can still be good to you! When you have this type of "still-yes" faith, you open yourself up to God in the form of "Yahweh." This is the God that lives

He Came Through Drippin'

outside of time. But what does Yahweh mean literally?

"Yahweh" is the Hebrew word for the self-revealed name of the God of the Old Testament. It comes from the Hebrew verb "To be." So, at its core, "Yahweh" means "To be." The English Bible translates it as "LORD," which distinguishes it from "Lord" (which is translated as "master"). So today, target your faith that God is the master of everything and needs nothing from you. Allow God to sit outside your moment of need or concern and praise him because HE IS "OUTSIDE OF TIME" STILL GOOD!

He Came Through Drippin'

What areas of your life do you need to keep the faith in?

What are some ways that God has been good to you during not-so-good times?

"Learn to become more faithful to God's yes than life's nos." – **C.S. Bailey**

He Came Through Drippin'

He Came Through Drippin'

Day 17
Finding Purpose in His Gifts

"Each of you should use whatever gift you have received to serve others, as faithful stewards of God's grace in its various forms." 1 Peter 4:10

Continuing our journey of faith and self-discovery, it's crucial to understand the impact of working from a place of purpose, leveraging the gifts that God has instilled in us. These gifts, given freely and without the intention of retraction, are our tools to navigate life's journey, serving others and fulfilling God's grand design. Reflect on your life's path and consider whether you're actively engaging with your divine gifts. Are you utilizing them to their fullest potential, or have they been

He Came Through Drippin'

sidelined? The distractions that lead us away from God's path are numerous, yet when we're deeply entrenched in working our gifts, there's little room for these diversions to take root. Today, challenge yourself to trust in the gift that God won't take back. Seek it, harness it, and express it. By doing so, you're not just keeping the faith; you're living it, actively participating in the divine flow of God's grace.

In 5-7 words describe your purpose.

Are you using your God-given gifts to their fullest potential?

What are some distractions in and around your life that keep you from fulfilling your purpose?

He Came Through Drippin'

"If you plan from purpose you won't need to ask God will your endeavors, be blessed because you started them with the blessing."
– **C.S. Bailey**

He Came Through Drippin'

He Came Through Drippin'

Day 18
Faith Beyond Our Understanding

"Then said Mary unto the angel, How shall this be, seeing I know not a man? 35 And the angel answered and said unto her, The Holy Ghost shall come upon thee, and the power of the Highest shall overshadow thee: therefore also that holy thing which shall be born of thee shall be called the Son of God. 36 And, behold, thy cousin Elisabeth, she hath also conceived a son in her old age: and this is the sixth month with her, who was called barren. 37 For with God nothing shall be impossible. 38 And Mary said, Behold the handmaid of the Lord; be it unto me according to thy word. And the angel departed from her." Luke 1:34-38 KJV

Today, let's dive deep into the essence of faith that goes beyond our understanding. In the story of Mary, we see a young woman faced with a divine plan that disrupts her life completely.

He Came Through Drippin'

Yet, her response, "Be it unto me according to thy word," reveals an extraordinary level of trust in God's alternate plans.

Just like Mary and Joseph, sometimes God asks us to set our lives, our plans, and our understanding aside to make way for His divine purpose. It's a reminder that our lives are not always about our immediate comfort or understanding but about being vessels for His greater plan.

This narrative challenges us to trust in God's alternate routes for our lives. It's a call to believe in His promises, even when they take us down paths we never anticipated. Mary's story is not just about the birth of Jesus; it's also about surrendering to God's plan, even when it contradicts our own.

As we approach the end of this month, let's reflect on the moments God has called us to trust in His alternate plans. Let's open our hearts to the possibilities that lie in saying, "Your will, not mine." Remember, God's plans may not always align with our ideals, but they always lead to our ultimate good and His greater glory.

What ideals do you have that you need to lay aside to find more clarity in God's will?

How can you surrender more to God today?

"We must cast our ideals to the side so we can find GOD'S ideas along the way."
- C.S. Bailey

He Came Through Drippin'

He Came Through Drippin'

He Came Through Drippin'

Day 19
There's a Place of Grace

"And we know that in all things God works for the good of those who love him, who have been called according to his purpose." Romans 8:28 NLT

Hey, what's up, Fam?

There was a time when I was overwhelmed with a lot I had to do, a lot of running around. I was doing this and that, but then, during a moment in prayer, I came across a thought I believe the Lord gave me. He said, "Chandler, everything you're in right now, I'm in right now." Today, I want you all to target your faith to trust in the fact that you're in the will of God. God's not going to give or provide you with a vision that drives you crazy or insane. So, don't be overwhelmed with doing the things of God to the point where you lose sight of His grace. There is a place of grace that God has for you, and I want you to target your faith toward finding and embracing that.

What are some places of grace in your life? (Relationships, Giftings, Physical Places).

List some areas of your life that you are currently overwhelmed with.

"Everything you're in right now I'm in right now." **- Holy Spirit**

He Came Through Drippin'

He Came Through Drippin'

Day 20
Finding Your Pace in God's Grace

"But they who wait for the Lord shall renew their strength; they shall mount up with wings like eagles; they shall run and not be weary; they shall walk and not faint." Isaiah 40:31 NLT

Yesterday, we talked about finding that place of grace. Today, I want to encourage you to discover the pace of grace. The term 'pace of grace' might not be new in theological circles, but Pastor Michael Todd's creative way of expressing it ministered to me deeply. There truly is a pace of grace. Sometimes, we rush the process, but today, be encouraged to have the faith to find your pace in God's grace.

He Came Through Drippin'

Reflect on Psalm 46:10, "Be still, and know that I am God," which reminds us of the importance of moving at God's pace, not ours. When you embrace this pace, you allow God's grace to flow over your work and everything you do. You're able to keep the faith while maintaining the right pace and pulse, without being overwhelmed by the process. Keep the Faith!

Write down some ways you can get better at patiently waiting on the Lord.

What area of your life are you most impatient in?

If anxiety was to peak its head, what area of your life would it be revealed?

> *"You're not just waiting on the Lord, you're waiting in the Lord, it's the pace of grace family."* - **C.S. Bailey**

He Came Through Drippin'

He Came Through Drippin'

Day 21
Joy of the Lord

Jesus was sleeping at the back of the boat with his head on a cushion. The disciples woke him up, shouting, "Teacher, don't you care that we're going to drown?"
39 When Jesus woke up, he rebuked the wind and said to the waves, "Silence! Be still!" Suddenly the wind stopped, and there was a great calm. 40 Then he asked them, "Why are you afraid? Do you still have no faith?" 41 The disciples were absolutely terrified. "Who is this man?" they asked each other. "Even the wind and waves obey him! Mark 4:35-41 NLT

Faith Fam, are there times you have felt weak? As you steward the dimensions of your capacity, I want you not to eliminate what God may be trying to elevate. God is resurfacing the demand that we, as His people, must genuinely place our trust in the Lord. However, this trust must not just be for things but for strength. Faith Fam, giving up quickly means you can do that; you've done it before. However, I believe you are sensing the demand in your life to press. So, today go to the Lord for renewed strength and ask God for more of him in what you are doing than more of you. Your next may not need a version of you with more strategy or might, but your next now may be more of the Lord's strength. So, today, target your faith for the renewed strength of the Lord in every area of your life. Keep the faith!

Write down a prayer asking God for renewed strength.

He Came Through Drippin'

Ask God to show you where you are working too hard in your life.

"Grace is more important than results. Find ways to stay in that space of grace for your race." - **C.S. Bailey**

He Came Through Drippin'

He Came Through Drippin'

Day 22
Think Higher!

Today, I want you to think about what you're thinking about. "Set your minds on things above, not on earthly things," as Colossians 3:2 instructs us. The reason I urge you to think of the things above is that sometimes, burdens are weighing you down. Challenges that make you feel less than what you truly are. But when you set your mind on things above, embracing the spirit of faith, you'll find your day naturally elevating. So, let's start our day by launching into God's love for us, being led by the Spirit, and trusting in faith that God has us in His hands. Keep The Faith!

He Came Through Drippin'

How have your thoughts been this month and week write them down and judge if they have been positive or negative ones

What are some practical ways you can rise above the frustrations and aggravations of life?

> *"Faith Fam you must learn how to think yourself clearly."* - **C.S. Bailey**

He Came Through Drippin'

He Came Through Drippin'

Day 23
Faith in God's Power, Not Ours

Today, I want you to target your faith toward a powerful truth from Zechariah 4:6 – "Not by might, nor by power, but by my Spirit, says the Lord of hosts." This scripture has been incredibly meaningful to me, especially in my current journey. The greater the exploits we accomplish, the more we realize our dependence on God. It's like with each success in God, He elevates us, and we find ourselves needing more of Him to manage what was created by Him, or to simply believe that we can do it because our entire life was orchestrated by Him.

He Came Through Drippin'

Some of you may be feeling this way today, and I want to assure you that you're not in a strange or wrong place. You're in a place of total dependence on God. What you're expecting God to do, expect Him to do it through you. And when you expect God to work through you, you'll need Him to remind you that He did it for you. Remember, it's not by your power or might, but by His Spirit. It's not in our strength but in His. Keep The Faith!

What are you expecting God to work through you?

"You don't need proof to know that HE's proven" – **C.S. Bailey**

He Came Through Drippin'

He Came Through Drippin'

Day 24
Reimagining God's Dreams

"Trust in and rely confidently on the Lord with all your heart And do not rely on your insight or understanding. In all your ways know and acknowledge and recognize Him, And He will make your paths straight and smooth [removing obstacles that block your way]."
Proverbs 3:5-6 AMP

I know this devotional is going to find you well because I can only imagine how important it is to keep the faith at the start of a fresh week. For today, I want to talk to you about dreaming again. Now, this isn't about your typical Disney dream. I'm talking about reconnecting with what God has already shown you, and imagining what God has in store for you. We need to use our creativity not just for new ideas,

He Came Through Drippin'

but to envision God's ideas. So today, be inspired from within. Trust what God has spoken, trust what God is saying now. Reimagine that vision and imagine what God has for you today. Reimagine the dream.

How can you tap into your creativity to envision God's ideas?

"He who pivots first gets paid first."
- C.S. Bailey

He Came Through Drippin'

He Came Through Drippin'

Day 25

Be a Promise Chaser: Go Beyond Feelings and Target Your Faith on God's Promises

Today, I want you to realize that you can be a man or woman after God's own heart. As it says in Acts 13:22, "After removing Saul, he made David their king. God testified concerning him: 'I have found David son of Jesse, a man after my own heart; he will do everything I want him to do.'"

Are you a promise chaser? Often, we chase paper, passions, or pursuits, but today let's aggressively go after God's promises for our lives. Being intentional is key. I know some

He Came Through Drippin'

days feel mundane, and you might not be in the mood to chase after God's word. Yet, today, let's focus our faith not on our feelings, but on our faith itself. It's time to "faith it"—that's right, F-A-I-T-H-I-N-G it—even through those times when you don't feel like it.

Are you truly a man or woman after God's own heart?

What can you do differently or better to go beyond your feelings and target your faith on the promises of God?

> *"It will be there when you get there"… my father* **Bishop Herbert Bailey**

He Came Through Drippin'

He Came Through Drippin'

Day 26
The Impossible is Possible

You crown the year with your bounty, and your carts overflow with abundance. Psalms 65:11 NIV

Nothing is impossible in God, but there are possibilities in life. What does it take, my friend, to reimagine the endless possibilities that are on the inside of you? Today don't just think that God can do anything; that's the easy part. However, I want you to consider that you can do the impossible in God.

Furthermore, not only does this take the limits off of God, but it takes the limits off of you. I genuinely believe the challenge lies not in what God can do; many of us have the faith that God

He Came Through Drippin'

can do anything but have the faith that God can do anything through you!

What are you believing God to do through you?

Whenever you think something is impossible always remember I-M possible!

"Legends are created in real-time."
- **C.S. Bailey**

He Came Through Drippin'

He Came Through Drippin'

Day 27
POSTURE IS EVERYTHING!

He prayed, "O Lord, God of Israel, there is no God like you in all heaven and earth. You keep your covenant and show unfailing love to all who walk before you in wholehearted devotion.
2 Chronicles 6:14 NLT

Faith Fam, our posture towards the things of God, is essential. One thing I can tell you about being in ministry and leadership in the body of Christ is that I meet many leaders with big goals defined as big wins for themselves in their service to God or the local church. It could be books, money, a lifestyle they desire to live, or simply a delicate desire for manifestation that comes from a pure motive in prayer.

He Came Through Drippin'

However, one thing I have learned about my faith in Jesus is no matter how rich or extensive of a stage you speak from, your influence, or your title in a denomination or community group. One thing is always required before the Lord, and that is the correct posture. So today, I want you to reflect on your posture toward the things of God, and even if it looks like your prayers, and desires are not being answered, please have faith, family, keep the proper posture before the Lord, and allow God to give you the desires of your heart.

How can you keep the proper posture before the Lord?

"Steward well what's not working well."

- C.S. Bailey

He Came Through Drippin'

He Came Through Drippin'

Day 28
The Interlock of Trust

"When I am afraid, I put my trust in you."
Psalm 56:3 NIV

Faith fam, it's easy to forget that God has blessings for you when you are concerned with the fear, not the faith attached to your storm. My desire today is that we would interlock our souls to trust God in everything we do. This includes the seasons of change and the shifts of life. However, to do this we must allow God's promises to prophesy into our lives. We do this by placing our trust in him and seeking the Lord when we are afraid. Seek God today!

He Came Through Drippin'

Write down 3 steps you would take to replace faith with fear in your current situation.

"If you focus up you will see above the fray." - **C.S. Bailey**

He Came Through Drippin'

He Came Through Drippin'

Day 29
TIME TO PURSUE!

The Lord looks down from heaven on the children of man, to see if there are any who understand, who seek after God. Psalms 14:2

It's time to seek God and pursue!

Faith Fam, it's time to pursue and seek God more than ever. Have you ever been desperate? Desperate for a change, to see God shift things in your life? When we pursue God, the imbalance of our decisions will collide with the purpose of God. When you are confused, seek God! I mean, seek God hard and run after His will for your life. When you allow the purpose of God to collide with the confusion of life. You

He Came Through Drippin'

will always come out with clear focus and strategic insight in the stormy seasons and battles that you may face in life!

What can you do differently in your day to ensure you make time to seek God more than ever?

Write down the things God has been speaking to your heart concerning your future.

"One word from God is all you need."
- **C.S. Bailey**

He Came Through Drippin'

He Came Through Drippin'

Day 30
The Legacy of Faith We Carry

"But after he had considered this, an angel of the Lord appeared to him in a dream, saying, Joseph, descendant of David, do not be afraid to take Mary as your wife, for the Child who has been conceived in her is of the Holy Spirit. 21 She will give birth to a Son, and you shall name Him Jesus (The Lord is salvation), for He will save His people from their sins. 22 All this happened in order to fulfill what the Lord had spoken through the prophet [Isaiah]: 23 "Behold, the virgin shall be with child and give birth to a Son, and they shall call His name Immanuel"—which, when translated, means, "God with us." 24 Then Joseph awoke from his sleep and did as the angel of the Lord had commanded him and took Mary as his wife, 25 but he kept her a virgin until she gave birth to a Son; and he named Him Jesus."
Matthew 1:20-25 AMP

He Came Through Drippin'

Today, let's reflect on the profound concept of 'The Word in the Bloodline' as highlighted in the birth story of Jesus. This narrative is not just about the miracle of the virgin birth; it's about the legacy and lineage of faith.

Joseph's and Mary's stories remind us that our journey of faith is often intertwined with the faith of those who came before us. God's plan for our lives is deeply rooted in a lineage that stretches beyond our immediate family, reaching back through generations.

When we celebrate the birth of Jesus, let's also honor the faith journey of those who came before us. Their prayers, their struggles, and their faith have paved the way for us. Our faith

He Came Through Drippin'

today is a testament to their legacy and a continuation of their spiritual journey.

As we approach the end of the year, let's be mindful of the spiritual heritage we carry. The faith we exercise today is not just for us but also for those who will come after us. Our faith stories will become part of a larger narrative that God is weaving through generations. Let's embrace this moment, recognizing that we are part of something much bigger than ourselves. Our faith, like that of Mary and Joseph, is contributing to a divine story that spans centuries.

He Came Through Drippin'

How can you make your desire for God more of a priority than what God can give you?

"Legends are created in real-time."

- C.S. Bailey

He Came Through Drippin'

He Came Through Drippin'

He Came Through Drippin'

He Came Through Drippin'

Thank you for reading my book, "The 30-Day Devotional, He Came Through Drippin'." I pray you are blessed each day, revisiting your notes, insights, and what God has spoken to you. As you reflect on the prompts and allow the scriptures to settle in your heart, may this book serve as a tool of meditation and guidance in your life. It seems fitting to close with a prayer.

Prayer

God, I am firstly thankful that this book has found its way into the readers' hands. I pray the words leaped from the pages to become visions within their hearts. Lord, I ask for an increase in areas of their lives where they struggle to seek Your guidance. Grant them vision for their journey, as they navigate life, lead their families, and impact their communities.

Father, instill in them a new vision rooted in You. I pray for healing in their bodies, minds, and spirits, and for clarity amidst confusion. May this book guide them,

He Came Through Drippin'

reminding them of Your peace—a peace that surpasses all understanding.

Father, I hope their walk with You has deepened through our time together in these pages. I pray for renewed hope, direction, and more. May Your presence bring them closer to love, teach them to lead with conviction, and move with assured faith in You, our Lord and Savior, Jesus Christ. Thank you for embarking on this journey with me. I look forward to connecting through future works and my website, www.ChandlerBailey.com, as part of Chandler Bailey Media Ministry. Your

He Came Through Drippin'

willingness to invest your time with us is greatly appreciated. Be blessed.

He Came Through Drippin'

www.ingramcontent.com/pod-product-compliance
Lightning Source LLC
Chambersburg PA
CBHW071147060526
44107CB00133B/337